BREAKING THE ~~GENERATIONAL~~ CURSE

MY JOURNEY TO BECOMING **DEBT FREE**

COREY A. HARRIS

BREAKING THE ~~GENERATIONAL~~ CURSE

MY JOURNEY TO BECOMING **DEBT FREE**

Copyright © 2021 by Corey A. Harris

All rights reserved. This book or any portion thereof may not be reproduced or used in any manner whatsoever without the express written permission of the publisher except for the use of brief quotations in a book review.

Limits of Liability and Disclaimer of Warranty

The author and publisher shall not be liable for your misuse of this material. This book is strictly for informational purposes. The purpose of this book is to educate and entertain. The author and publisher do not guarantee anyone following these techniques, suggestions, tips, ideas, or strategies will become successful. The author and publisher shall have neither liability nor responsibility to anyone with respect to any loss or damage caused, or alleged to be caused, directly or indirectly by the information contained in this book. Views expressed in this publication do not necessarily reflect the views of the publisher.

Printed in the United States of America
Keen Vision Publishing, LLC
www.keen-vision.com
ISBN: 978-1-948270-86-1

For my supportive family, my beautiful mother, Bernadette; my grandfather, John Lee; my late step grandmother, Arleane; my grandmother, Jean; my sister, NaTasha; and my nephews, King JaCorey & Jayden

TABLE OF CONTENTS

Introduction	9
Chapter One: Humble Beginnings	13
Chapter Two: Collecting the Debt	17
Chapter Three: Hello, Workforce!	21
Chapter Four: Joining the Air Force	25
Chapter Five: More Debt, More Problems	29
Chapter Six: My First Deployment	33
Chapter Seven: New Job Me, Please	37
Chapter Eight: My Life Coach	41
Chapter Nine: Everything Must Go	45
Chapter Ten: What Now?	49
Chapter Eleven: Snowballing Debt with Setbacks	53
Chapter Twelve: Tackling Debt in a Pandemic	57
Chapter Thirteen: The Road Less Traveled	59
Meet the Author	63
Stay Connected	65

INTRODUCTION

We all have that one goal or dream we hope to one day accomplish. Some people believe in themselves enough to know that they can have anything they put their minds to. That's amazing, but I didn't write this book for those individuals. This book is for those who feel that their background, rural upbringing, or environment keep them from living out their dreams. I wrote this book for the individuals who have experienced so much failure that they no longer believe success is possible for them. This book was written for people who want to believe, but they don't see enough successful people who can relate to what they are going through. I wrote this book for the person who has made so many mistakes and bad decisions, they can't see their way out. This book is for the person who feels like every time they make one step forward, they get knocked three steps back. If you fit any of these descriptions, this book is just for you.

I spent the early part of my adult years in college, studying for my undergraduate and graduate degrees. These degrees were not cheap, and the Pell Grants and few scholarships I received were not enough to cover the cost of tuition, books, fees, and my basic necessities. Student loans were my only choice, and they costed me greatly. In addition to student loan debt, my desire for instant gratification landed me with over $200k in financial debt. I was working four jobs to pay bills. Needless to say, my life was stressful and unfruitful. One day, I took a hard look in the mirror and realized that this was not the life I wanted to live or pass on to the next generation. I decided to make significant lifestyle changes to create a life I could be proud of — this included becoming debt-free.

This book, *Breaking the Generational Curse: My Journey to Becoming Debt Free,* sheds light on how I became debt-free. For the first time, I will unfold the many challenges I faced along my journey to financial freedom and how I overcame each obstacle to reach my goal. After you read this book, my prayer is that you will be inspired to pursue your goals relentlessly, no matter what you may encounter along your journey.

As the saying goes, *"Life is what you make it."* You own the creative rights to your life — not your past, debt, income, or circumstances. Your life is defined solely by your choices. You already knew that, but I wrote this book just in case you needed a reminder. After you read the final page, I hope you are inspired to be the person you needed when you were younger. Let the change you want to see start in you. Where you are right now is a result of who you were, but where you go depends entirely on who you choose to be!

INTRODUCTION

Telling my story wasn't an easy task, but I thought about you as I wrote this book. I wanted you to know that not only can you become debt-free, but you can achieve any goal you desire. Much like many of the goals people aspire to achieve, being debt-free isn't just something you hear about on TV or social media. Every day, regular people just like you and I are becoming debt-free and later millionaires. No matter who you are or your current circumstance, you can become the individual you desire to be.

Chapter One
HUMBLE BEGINNINGS

Before we get into how I became debt-free, you must understand my upbringing. Unlike many of the people you hear about becoming debt-free, making major investments, and later becoming millionaires, I wasn't born with a silver spoon in my mouth. There weren't millions of dollars waiting on me to turn 21. I didn't have some filthy rich family member who left behind investments that would carry me into my old age. I had very humble beginnings.

Born in Montgomery, Alabama, and raised in Highland Home, Alabama, I grew up in a single-family home and was reared by my mom. My father was not around, so my mother was left with the burden of raising my sister and me alone. As a child, I watched her sacrifice so much, working tirelessly to provide and support my sister and me. Without question, I inherited my work ethic and motivation from her. According to my grandparents, I inherited much more than that, as they often joke that I am the male replica of my mother.

My mom and I are eighteen years apart, eighteen years and two weeks to be exact. I was born before she graduated high school. Despite the hardships she encountered raising two kids alone, my mother remains the most caring, loving, strong, and selfless woman I know. She has the purest of hearts, always willing to lend a helping hand.

Throughout my childhood, my mother always taught me to treat people good and good things would come my way. Treating people with respect was a must for my mother. She did not tolerate any level of disrespect and always ensured my sister and I used our manners. I was rarely punished, but when she did finally punish me, it was for old things I thought she'd forgotten about, in addition to any new mishaps.

I may be biased, but my mother prepares the best meals. Every meal was a complete orgasm for my tastebuds; I always had to have at least two plates of whatever she prepared. Naturally, I desired to learn to cook like her, and she taught me everything I needed to know.

Like most children who grew up in single-parent households, my sister and I had responsibilities to help my mother keep the house in order. My chores were cooking, cleaning, and doing laundry. In addition to teaching us to be responsible, my mother enforced a relationship with God. There was no such thing as missing Bible class, choir practice, Sunday school, or regular church service in my mother's household. If she did not take me, she made sure I went. The values she instilled in me at a young age are the core values I still live by today.

Over time, my mother taught me so much. Unfortunately, she could not teach me how to be a man. Since my father was absent, my grandfather assumed the role of my father. I spent as much time as I could with him, and he would teach me how to be a man. My grandfather made sure I knew how to use my hands to do things around the house like cutting the grass, trimming trees, making repairs, etc. I was pretty good at everything he taught me, but I hated getting my hands dirty. After we completed a task, I would rush to wash my hands. There was something about having dirty hands that never sat well with me.

One day, my grandfather asked me how I planned to make a living. "Do you want to use your hands or your head?" he asked.

"You know what, grandaddy, I have not thought about that," I replied. "That gives me something to think about, especially since I do not like getting my hands dirty." After some thought, I later informed my grandfather that I wanted to use my head and go to college.

I attended Highland Home School in rural Crenshaw County. My grandmother was my bus driver, and after she retired, my mom became my bus driver. Acting up in school was a no go, as my teachers would threaten to walk with me to the bus at dismissal. My high school GPA was above average, and I was among the top 25 students in my graduating class of 2008. I had many scholarships and colleges to chose from, but deciding on a program to pursue was difficult. I excelled in my high school Agriculture (Ag) class, so my Ag teacher suggested that I research Alabama A&M University's (AAMU) Agricultural Science Program.

Chapter Two
COLLECTING THE DEBT

Without hesitation, I researched The College of Agricultural, Life, and Natural Sciences at AAMU. I was amazed by what I found and instantly made Alabama A&M my choice to pursue a degree in agriculture. During my last semester in high school, I was excited to start my college career. The thought of being a first-generation college student was so humbling.

Though I was thrilled to be the first in my family to attend college, I didn't know what to expect. My research showed me that college was expensive, but I did not realize how expensive it would be. In addition to tuition, I had to figure out how I would pay for books, fees, room, and board. I qualified for the Pell Grant and a small scholarship, but they didn't cover the cost. During my first semester, I had some serious decisions to make. I still had an outstanding balance on the first day of class, and if I didn't pay it, my classes would have been dropped, and I would have been on my way back to Highland Home. The only option remaining was student loans.

Reluctantly, I signed the promissory note for the first loan of my first semester of school. I continued that same process every semester after.

I lived on campus my freshman and sophomore year, and during my junior year, I moved to the Normal Hills Campus Apartments. My refund checks each semester covered my rent for the remainder of the semester. During the summers, I managed to land great internships with the United States Department of Agriculture. Those internships exposed me to many opportunities in my chosen career field and allowed me to make money during the summer. I had no money management skills or financial literacy, so using my income to my advantage was not a thing. I used my money however I saw fit, mostly to meet my needs and do some of the things I wanted to do.

On December 9, 2011, I graduated Cum Laude with a Bachelor of Science in Agricultural Science. After graduation, I pondered what I would do next. Before my senior year in undergrad, I began getting some orthodontic work done for my teeth. Well, my orthodontic treatment extended far past my graduation date, and I needed to stay in Huntsville, AL at least 12 more months or pay another orthodontic to finish the remainder of my treatment. My treatment had been paid in full, and I figured it would be mindless to pay again. So I decided to stay in Huntsville, AL, and pursue a master's.

Months before graduation, I had been toiling with the idea of applying for graduate school. I battled with this decision because I knew that a master's degree would mean more debt, long hours of studying, research papers, defending a thesis, etc. Additionally, there were so many options to choose from, and I wasn't sure what I wanted to do. Nervous, scared, and afraid, I applied to AAMU Graduate Studies Agribusiness Program. I did very well in the Agriculture Science undergraduate program, so I knew I had a strong chance of being accepted as a graduate student.

When I finally received my acceptance letter from the program, I was excited at first. My excitement was short lived, as my acceptance letter also included a list of things I would need to get started on my journey to earning my master's degree. Tuition, books, and fees for graduate school is much more expensive than undergraduate school. Graduate school tuition was approximately $10K per semester. I found myself at a standstill because I was already over $40K in student loan debt from my undergraduate degree. There were some tuition assistance programs for graduate students. However, it was challenging to get with all the budget and funding cuts. If I wanted my master's, I would have to come up with a solution quickly.

Unfortunately, time was not on my side. Without financial support, I had no choice but to take out another loan to further my education. Going into debt for my education was considered good debt, or so I thought. As each semester went by, I signed more promissory notes, accumulating more student loan debt. As I focused on my graduate program, I lost sight of my debt accumulation. It kept racking up until December 13, 2013, when I graduated with a Master of Science in Agribusiness. I had always envisioned that my proudest academic achievement would be when I walked across the stage, wearing my master's hood as the dean announced my merits to all who had gathered to watch. At that moment, I realized my proudest achievement was not graduation day; it was the academic achievement itself. The fact that I studied diligently made me proud. I could have quit when the going got tough, or the money wasn't enough. I didn't. I kept working to achieve my goals. When working on campus didn't bring in enough money to support my lifestyle, I worked off campus at JCPenney and later, Publix Supermarket, all while maintaining an impeccable GPA.

As I reflected on my academic career, I started to feel an overwhelming amount of pride about everything I'd accomplished and endured to achieve my goals. In addition to the great program I mastered, my internships and real-life experiences during my college days undoubtedly shaped my world views and made me a better person.

In addition to working hard, I also made sure I had fun! Throughout my undergraduate and graduate career at AAMU, I attended my fair share of fraternity and sorority parties. I also attended as many athletic events as possible, particularly the football and basketball games. I pledged Sigma Tau Epsilon, Professional Fraternity, Rho Chapter, and later pledged Alpha Phi Alpha Fraternity, Incorporated, Delta Theta Lambda Chapter. I had a remarkable experience at AAMU. However, when I left with my master's degree, a whopping $72K in student loan debt followed closely behind me.

Chapter Three

HELLO, WORKFORCE!

During my last semester of graduate school at AAMU, I didn't have classes every day, so I moved back home and commuted four hours to the university whenever my instructor required in-person assignments. While at home, I worked as a substitute teacher and substitute bus driver at my old high school. I found myself following in my mother's footsteps, wanting to become a school bus driver. Though I had an undergraduate degree and was working on a master's, I wasn't entirely clear on my purpose. The more I substituted at my high school, the more I realized that helping others and teaching was something I found joy in. I knew then that my passion was to be in the classroom, teaching and mentoring our youth. My passion led me right into my purpose.

While substitute teaching, I spent as much time as possible with my high school Agriculture teacher, Tony Johnson (Mr. J). Mr. J taught me his classroom and shop techniques. He also taught me his methods of classroom management and how he handled behavior. Mr. J was loved and respected by his colleagues and students. All students thoroughly enjoyed his shop and classroom projects. Unfortunately for Highland High, Mr. J was set to retire the semester after I would graduate with my master's degree.

When the time came, and Mr. J was finally retiring, I hoped to fill his spot as the Ag teacher. The position posted on the Alabama State Department of Education website, and I applied immediately. After my application was reviewed and I was offered an interview for the job. There were other qualified candidates as well; however, I was the only candidate who had been working in the school system and was an alumnus of the school. When I did not get the job, I was devasted. However, I was not defeated. When the position became available again, I applied again. This time, I interviewed at the Central Office, but I never received a response. I later found out that a football coach who had no experience or degree in Agriculture was given the position. Neither of my degrees was in education, but I had an agriculture background. My experience was not classroom-related but more real-world and hands-on. I thought I would be a shoo-in for the position, but that was not the case.

Eventually, I stopped driving the school bus and substitute teaching at Highland Home School and moved to Montgomery Public Schools. I drove the bus as a swing driver. A swing driver works every day but usually drives different routes, depending on who is out sick. I drove my first bus route at Dunbar Ramer School in south Montgomery County. I had been driving for months and soon realized that a school bus driver's salary would not support me or my debt that was accruing daily interest.

Around this time, Apple launched their iPhone 5. I went to Verizon on Ann Street in Montgomery for an upgrade. While there, I ran into an old friend, David Wallace, who was the store manager. He asked me if I wanted a job, and I was like, "Hell yeah! I need a job bad, bro."

"Well, think about the working here on your way home and let me know," David replied. "I would love to have you on my team."

After giving it some thought, I reached out to David and took him up on the offer. He sent me the link, I applied, and almost instantly, I got a phone call from corporate inviting me to interview.

The interview went extremely well, and I was hired. I continued to drive the school bus every morning before my shift at Verizon. On my off days from Verizon, I drove mornings, afternoons, and for field trips during the day for extra income. At this point, I had multiple sources of income and was making the minimum payment on my student loan debt. Even though I enjoyed receiving the commission pay every month in addition to my hourly pay from Verizon, sales soon became a burden, and I no longer enjoyed it. I began to feel a negative, evil spirit when I went to work. I knew that something had to change.

My grandfather's wife became ill with ovarian cancer, and her illness became a burden on my grandfather. My step-grandmother had been the lady of the house. She took care of all the budgeting of bills, meals, cleaning, keeping the house in order, etc. This cancer attacked her body quickly, and she was unable to continue doing those things. I knew I needed to do something to help, so I moved in with my grandparents to help lighten the load while continuing to drive the bus and work at Verizon.

My step-grandmother had been like a mother to me and I hated that she was in such a bad condition. When she transitioned and gained her angel wings, I went into a deep state of depression. I took leave from Verizon and eventually decided to resign and drive the school bus full-time. I felt at ease, and less stressed driving the school bus, which was necessary as I battled depression. I did not seek help for my depression. Honestly, I was afraid and didn't know how to explain what I was dealing with. During this time, I started working out, getting physically fit. Working out and doing cardio brought me out of depression. I felt different once my eating habits changed. My physique started changing, and I loved the results. I fell in love with physical fitness, and it has since become part of my daily lifestyle.

Then, I had a thought. Why not join the military and get paid to stay in shape? Also, joining the military seemed like a great way to pay off my student loan debt. I did some research and began pursuing a career in the military.

Chapter Four

JOINING THE AIR FORCE

If you didn't know, military recruiters have a way with words. They say the right things to get recruits to sign those documents and enlist right away. After I did my research, I realized the United States Air Force was the only way to go for me. The Air Force would not pay my student loan debt, but I would get a $20k signing bonus to offset my student loan debt. On June 6, 2015, as I was preparing to be sworn in as a newly enlisted airman in the 187th Alabama Air National Guard at Dannelly Field in Montgomery, my recruiter approached me with bad news. The $20k signing bonus was null and void due to budget cuts made effective the previous day.

Was I mad? Mad was an understatement. I was looking forward to that bonus for my student loans. I enlisted anyway because I knew something positive would come from being in the Air Force.

The dream of becoming an Agriculture teacher had been

slowly fading away. I became concerned that I went into debt for nothing because I was not utilizing those degrees. One day, I found out that the Agriculture Science teacher at Dunbar Ramer School, the school I had been driving the bus at, would be retiring. I knew I qualified and that this was my time to finally become an AgriScience Teacher.

When the position was posted on the Alabama State Department of Education website, I didn't have to do much work. My profile was current and up to date from applying for a position at my high school. I applied and was scheduled to interview with the principal of Dunbar one morning after my bus route.

The principal was very impressed with me and unaware that he had a candidate driving the bus. During my interview, I explained to the principal that I had enlisted in the Air Force and would be out of town for basic training until fall. The principal looked at me and said, "What God has for you is for you! Do well at your training, and I will see you in the fall in the classroom." At that very moment, I almost shouted, "HALLELUJAH! THANK YOU GOD!" right in the middle of his office.

I arrived at basic training nervous, anxious, excited, but ready to get it over. Little did I know, I had very little in common with most of the guys in my flight. Most of them had never been away from home. There were about three guys in our entire training class who were older than me.

Basic training was a breeze. Unlike most of the fellows, I was never worried about the military training instructors — I knew it was more mental than physical. People often asked why I enlisted instead of going in as an officer. Enlisting allowed me to gain more experience and income as I studied for the officer's exam. Becoming an officer in the Air Force is rather challenging because many airmen have degrees. Officers must wait to be selected for specific career fields. You could be waiting months, a year, or longer. Taking the officer's AFOQT is also no easy task. Though I began studying for it, I struggled to remain focused. I decided I was not going to continue studying for the exam and would finish my military career enlisted.

Upon graduating from basic training, I went straight into technical training for my career field. My job as an Aircraft Armament Apprentice Specialist was to inspect missile rail launchers and bomb racks and install and uninstall the Gatling gun on the F-16 Fighting Falcon Aircraft. After completing my technical training, I returned home to my base to start on the job training. Just before graduation, I found myself looking at houses online. I was not set on buying a house, but I was certainly preparing. While doing on-the-job training for the military and preparing to set up my first classroom, I found myself talking to some of the guys in my shop who were new homeowners.

Chapter Five

MORE DEBT, MORE PROBLEMS

Fall 2016 arrived, and I was excited to start teaching middle school AgriScience at Dunbar Ramer. Even though I had two degrees, I needed a teacher certification in order to teach. So, I applied for a one-year emergency teaching certificate and enrolled in online education courses at Athens State University. I took two classes per semester for three semesters, tuition paid by Air Force. I thought to myself, "Why didn't you join the military a long time ago? You could have BEEN debt-free! After successfully completing my courses at Athens and passing the PRAXIS exam, I became a certified teacher.

The idea of owning a home was at the forefront of my mind. It was just my luck that one of the homes I'd been looking at was within the school district. The house owner was actually one of the guys I drove the bus with before going to basic training. Master's level salary for first-year teachers was $42k. That wasn't a lot of money, but I was determined to make it work. I visited the house and immediately fell in love. It was my dream house, and I had to have it.

The property had 5.5 acres, and the house was a sight to see. It had a detached three-car garage with two doors, 1457 sq. ft. that included three bedrooms, two bathrooms, and a beautiful back porch patio. The home was built at the end of a private road, and it could all be mine for $139,900. It was just me, no wife or kids, but I had to have this property. I did not qualify for the VA loan because I had not deployed yet. My credit score was in the high 700's, and I was ready to apply for my first home loan. I met all the requirements and deadlines pending the underwriter's review. When I received my first teacher paycheck of $3674.25 gross pay, I didn't even think about what I would do with my first check. I submitted it to the underwriter, my loan was approved, and I was clear to close on my new home. I saved roughly $10k, and I should have used that towards my debt. Instead, I paid 7% at closing with more than $131,000 left in debt.

Exhausting most of my savings to buy the home, I used what was left to buy some necessities for the house. I wasn't bringing in enough income to live comfortably, so I survived paycheck to paycheck and used a credit card for the things I needed until I got paid at the end of the month. I paid the credit card in full every month, but I hated the idea of not having a savings account. Eventually, I was able to build a decent savings account again. I wasn't able to rebuild my savings on my teacher and Air National Guard income alone. Luckily, I had kept my school bus certification up to date because I knew I would need it again. Many coaches do not have CDL's to drive a bus for extracurricular activities, so I drove the bus to athletic games at my school and other schools within the county. That extra cash went directly into my savings account.

Chapter Six

MY FIRST DEPLOYMENT

When school closed for summer break, I worked on base as a temp technician, doing my drill status job and preparing for my first deployment downrange. I still received my teacher pay monthly and was receiving bi-weekly payments from base. My finances were great, and I had paid all of my bills six months in advance, except for the mortgage. I could only pay the mortgage in advance for up to two months. I had a decent savings account and still made the minimum payment on my student loans.

Just before Halloween 2017, I was deployed to Ahmad al-Jaber Air Base in Kuwait. Many veterans will say Kuwait is not a deployment, but my Certificate of Release of Active Duty (DD-2214) says otherwise. This was my first time traveling outside of the United States, and I didn't know what to expect. Being overseas during Thanksgiving and Christmas holidays was not too bad, as I deployed with my cousin, Darius Chambers. Darius and I grew up together, went to the same school, played baseball and basketball, rode bikes, went swimming, got in trouble, and got our asses whooped together. His birthday is four days before mine, and he is one year younger than me. Before I joined the military, I often asked him about his job and experience. Darius made my transition into the military easy — he was my go-to person.

While I was on active duty status, my student loans were deferred. The student loan payments that I had been making went directly into my savings. With this extra money sitting in my savings account, I began to desire something nice for myself. I felt like I deserved a reward for how hard I'd been working.

Buying a luxury car was something I often dreamed of but never thought would happen. While out on base, I ran across a Military AutoSource banner. Military AutoSource provides the most comprehensive vehicle buying programs for overseas U.S. military members. This program gave military members access to exclusive benefits and savings. For several weeks, I would visit the website daily, researching the car I wanted. The 2018 Mercedes-Benz CLA 250 caught my attention. It would be manufactured and customized in Germany and shipped to me in America within six months. As I designed my car and researched my options, I was stoked!

Military Autosource got me approved instantly with a low APR. I submitted my order, and it was approved and submitted. Though I was excited to enjoy my new ride, I accrued $46k more in debt. As I think back on it, it was absolutely crazy to make monthly payments on a car I wouldn't be able to drive for six months.

Now that I was $250k in debt, I knew I had to figure out

a way to generate more income to pay down my debt. My military and teacher income would not suffice. My mom was driving for a charter bus company at the time, and they needed more drivers. So again, following her footsteps, I applied to drive charter buses with Cline Tours, Inc. and was hired.

When I returned to America, I had four jobs. I taught Monday through Friday, drove the school bus to athletic events during the week, went to Unit Training Assembly (drill) one weekend a month, and drove charter buses every other weekend. The only time I would visit my mom was when we had mother-son duo charters. We spent time together as we worked. At this point, I was working for money and giving it away to debt. I spent more time away from my dream home than actually living in it.

Chapter Seven

NEW JOB ME, PLEASE

Surviving my first year of teaching was challenging; however, the second year was even more challenging. Many days, I got so frustrated that I wanted to throw in the towel and walk out. You must have passion and patience to teach middle school students because the money is certainly not enough to be motivated. By year two, teaching was becoming a burden, and the passion I had to pour into children was diminishing. I knew it was time for a change when Hennessey on the rocks was my drink of choice at 3:30 in the afternoon. I was drinking every afternoon at home to relax. Previously, drinking had been something I enjoyed occasionally, not daily. I quickly realized that it was an unhealthy way of dealing with the stress, so I put the Hennessy down and started doing cardio every afternoon. Working out and staying healthy kept me level-headed. Throughout that second year of teaching, I began to entertain the idea of overseas contracting. Contractors usually work with the military, sometimes doing the same job, but compensated ten times more. Contracting would be the only way I would be able to afford my brand-new Mercedes-Benz and support my lifestyle.

My brand-new Mercedes-Benz was delivered just a couple of weeks before the end of the school year. Excitement set in as I was finally able to enjoy the car I had been making monthly payments on for six months. At this point, I had three vehicles, and two of them were paid off. Having three vehicles meant I had extra bills for maintenance, insurance, and gas. This also made it hard to choose which car I wanted to drive daily. Now that I had all of this materialistic stuff, I had to secure a contracting job overseas. Going overseas would allow me the opportunity to network and eventually land a six-figure job. I kept my goal in the forefront of my mind and applied for seven to ten requisitions daily.

A company in Afghanistan reached out to me about an armed security guard position. I had applied for so many jobs I didn't even recall applying for this role. Additionally, I had heard so many horror stories about Afghanistan from Darius and others that I was afraid to accept the offer. The armed security position paid $60k a year with 30 days of vacation. After much contemplation, I accepted the offer. My third year of school rapidly approached, but I knew I had to resign from the classroom to start my contracting career. Completing the paperwork, background check, and security clearance verification took a few weeks, so I had some time to prepare a formal resignation. After I submitted my resignation, I was ready to start my contracting career overseas.

I was stationed in Kabul, Afghanistan, at Hamid Karzai

International Airport military base. Working as an armed security guard afforded me the opportunity to network with many other contractors. Most of them were retired military or current national guardsmen. I served as a Senior Armed Security Guard, and this job required sensitive area access, armed escorts throughout the flight line, Tower and Entry Control Point functions, and roving patrols. Every day, I carried a loaded M9 with two spare clips and a loaded M4 with six magazines. I worked six 12-hour days with one off-day and got paid bi-weekly. I devoted every paycheck to paying towards the principal on my mortgage, car loan, and the rest of my bills at home. One day while on post, I read the book *Rich Dad Poor Dad* by Robert Kiyosaki. *Rich Dad Poor Dad* is about Robert Kiyosaki and his two dads-his birth father (poor dad) and his best friend's father (rich dad). He shares ways in which both men changed his views on money and investing. This book opened my eyes to so much about money and investing. I was slow-witted when it came to finances, and I needed to change expeditiously. I did not know anything about investing, but I was willing to learn.

Chapter Eight

MY LIFE COACH

At this point, you are probably wondering, "When does Corey finally stop buying things, getting new jobs, and start focusing on becoming debt-free?" Well, after reading that book, I was jolted to take a more serious approach to tackling my debt. Do you remember my friend, David from Verizon? Well, he played an integral role in my journey to becoming debt-free. During my early teenage years, cellphones became popular. After a little convincing, my mother finally decided to purchase me a cellphone. She always worked with the same person when buying phones. One day, she finally introduced me to her sales consultant, David Wallace. I met David at the beginning of his career. Little did I know, David would someday become my boss and friend and play a role in my journey to becoming debt-free.

Before leaving home to contract overseas, I joined Gold's Gym. Gold's had the best military membership rate and was the closest to my house. I worked out after school and anytime during the summer. David became my accountability gym partner. David motivated me and pushed me to reach my fitness goals. After each workout, we would sit in the steam room and converse about our short/long term goals. David has a Bachelor of Science in Finance and a Master of Business Administration in General Business. From his experiences, he could do numbers in his sleep. He would often ask questions about my finances, but I was not comfortable discussing my income/finances. Deep down, I knew I needed to have that conversation someday to get out of debt.

After reading *Rich Dad Poor Dad,* I listened to the audiobook of *The Total Money Makeover* by Dave Ramsey. *The Total Money Makeover* tells you how to stop accepting debt as normal, eliminate it forever in small increments, and build the financial future you deserve in seven steps. This audiobook was terrific! It was more personal and spoke directly to my debt situation.

That audiobook made me realize just how financially illiterate I was. I had been making poor financial decisions my entire life. It was time to reevaluate how I spent money and make some serious changes. That would require me to revise how I viewed money and stop enabling others by giving them money. For years, I'd been spending my earnings on materialistic things I wasn't even enjoying, so it only made sense to sell everything. David had been telling me all along that if I planned on contracting overseas long term, I should sell everything. It's not like I would be there to use any of my assets anyway. I knew he was right. However, I was concerned about selling my house. The house had become my only place of peace when I was home. I wondered, "If something happened and I needed to move back home for an extended time, what would I do?" Staying with family or David was an option, but being an introvert made this thought challenging. David ensured me that we would figure something out when that time came. Holding on to my house was no longer an option. If I was going to become debt-free, I had to say goodbye to my dream home...at least for now.

Contracting can be tricky. You could wake up any day and be without a job. Well, that is precisely what happened to me. One day, I was informed that my job was up for bid, and the new contract would require myself and others to be displaced. With this new information, I decided to rely on my networking skills. I emailed HR about an open vacancy with another company. HR responded with the link to apply. The salary for this contract was $90k a year with 14-30 days of vacation. I applied, had a phone interview, and was hired.

Before leaving Kabul, I decided to sell the Mercedes-Benz. This car had been sitting in my garage months at a time, and I would not let anyone drive it. I would start the engine from Afghanistan over Wi-Fi using the Mercedes Me app on my phone. There were cameras around my property, and I could see when the car would start. After eight minutes, the engine would automatically shut off. In order to sell this car, I would need to give David power of attorney.

David gave me insight on who to reach out to once I was ready to sell my house. I was not attached to the new car, I only had it two months before I left for Afghanistan, but the house was different. I had this property for two years, and I was very much attached to it. Deciding to sell the house was not easy. After days of thinking and looking at my new budget without the house and bills, I was ready to make the decision. I called David to let him know I was prepared to sell my home. David said, "You know what to do. Call my wife and tell her you are ready!" Without hesitation, I called his wife, Sarah Rose Wallace, with Wallace and Moody Realty to tell her I was ready to sell.

As you get older, you realize there are only a few people you can genuinely trust, count on, and confide in. David is one of those people for me. Even though I am across the globe, we still make time to give each other good counsel. We challenge each other to be the best versions of ourselves. When I am home, we worship together. Through the years, he became an acquaintance, a colleague, a friend, and now a brother.

Iron sharpens iron; so a man sharpens the countenance of his friend.

Proverbs 27:17 (AMP)

Chapter Nine
EVERYTHING MUST GO

A few weeks later, I resigned from my job in Afghanistan and boarded a plane back to America. Christmas was approaching within a few days, and I wanted to be home with my family. I had missed the previous Thanksgiving and Christmas because of my deployment to Kuwait. I was so happy that I got to pop in and surprise my family just days before Christmas. My new position would start on January 7, 2019, and this gave me just over two weeks to prepare my house to be put on the market and sell my car. While at home, I spent some time comparing my budgets with and without the house and car. What I saw was ridiculous. As a single man, there was no reason I should have been spending money the way I did.

2019 budget with house & car
    $802 mortgage
    $656 car payment
    $120 cell phone

$145 car insurance
$110 life insurance
$86 student loans (minimum payment)
$75 internet
$55 electricity
$40 Tricare selective reserve insurance
$18 water
$51 alarm monitoring
$200 groceries
$100 restaurants
$100 gas
$100 misc.
$2,658 monthly
$31,896 annually

2019 budget without house & car
$120 cell phone
$110 life insurance
$86 student loan (minimum payment)
$40 Tricare selective reserve insurance
$356 monthly
$4,272 annually
$27,624 annual savings

By selling everything, I would be saving $27k a year. I could use that $27k to pay down my student loan debt. My student loans had many different interest rates, and the interest rates were based on when the loans were disbursed while I was in college. With my new budget, I could eventually start making larger payments and get rid of the debt quicker. To sell the 2018 Mercedes-Benz CLA 250 (the biggest liability I had),

I needed to pay the loan off in full to get the title. I applied for a personal loan for $30k and was approved. That resulted in me being $280k in debt, but not for long. I paid the car loan off and positioned myself to sell the car.

On January 6, 2019, I left the house that I had loved for the last two years for the last time. I also left the good-for-nothing Mercedes-Benz parked in the garage for the last time, but again, I didn't care too much about that car. My flight to Yuma, Arizona, was early the next morning. I spent the night with my mom, and she dropped me off at the airport. That evening, I was very emotional as I walked away from everything I had worked so hard for. Additionally, the thought of being so far away from my family again made the situation even worse.

Sarah Rose Wallace made selling my house a breeze. She put in the extra time and effort to get my house listed and sold in my absence, might I add, quickly too. The house was under contract within a week of listing. We met every deadline thanks to her attention to detail and expertise. She worked fast and even took care of my inspection report issues. I did not have to make any phone calls, solicit quotes, or do any follow-ups. She took care of it all. She even hired a professional photographer to come out and take professional photos. She made the process of selling my house super easy! Days after Sarah sold the house, David sold the car at an auction for $25k. The car had less than 3k miles, with the initial cost at $46k. I lost $21k upon selling this car due to depreciated value. I barely broke even by selling them both. I also sold my other two vehicles and used the money to pay off other debt, bringing my debt total to just over $85k.

Chapter Ten

WHAT NOW?

I was deployed to Camp Taji in Iraq outside of Baghdad and later moved to Qayyarah Air Base (Q West) with my new military contracting company as a Field Engineer. My responsibilities were to lead aerostat efforts. I was now homeless and carless by choice, basically with no bills. As my savings account stacked up, I wondered what to do with all the extra income. Invest or pay off student loan debt, invest 50% of my income, pay off debt with the other 50%, invest my income, or pay off my debt? Investing was new to me; I researched as much as I could before giving it a shot.

Investing in the stock market can be short term and long term, and the stock market can be bullish or bearish. A bull market is on the rise and economically sound, while a bear market is receding, and the stocks are losing value. My portfolio was diverse. I bought penny stocks and a few regular stocks. Penny stocks are common shares of public companies that trade for less than one dollar per share. Regular stocks were more expensive per share. I knew I wanted to buy stocks as often as possible, so I researched the stock market daily and learned about Bitcoin one day. Bitcoin is a cryptocurrency, innovative payment network, a new kind of money. It is digital money that is instant, private, and free from bank fees. Bitcoin is extremely volatile. Bitcoin went from $0.06 per bitcoin in April 2017 to over $19k per bitcoin in December 2017. That was an over 18,000% increase in eight months.

Bitcoin price dropped tremendously to $5,134 per bitcoin. If I did not buy, I would lose out on the opportunity to own a bitcoin. Without further hesitation, I bought one whole bitcoin. Every day at several times throughout the day, I would check the price of bitcoin. Every day the price would increase. I was excited about making money with this cryptocurrency. The price increased to over $12k in just three months. I knew I'd tapped into a gold mine! I invested more time researching the volatility of Bitcoin and watching the price. Suddenly, the price started falling, and it dropped below $10k. I immediately sold my Bitcoin and took my profit of $4k. This all happened within four months.

I was stuck between continuing to invest or working on snowballing student loan debt. I was fired up and wanted to invest more, but I knew that in order to experience real financial freedom, I needed to handle that last bit of debt.

On June 10, 2019, I joined the Flight Crew. The company offered full benefits with matching contributions for 401k, tuition assistance, perks at work, etc. I was offered a nice six-figure salary to basically be a drone pilot. The training was intense! Can you imagine processing at least five months' worth of work, knowledge, and information in a matter of eight weeks? Though it was difficult, all the debt I had was my motivation to complete the course.

Once I got the class out of the way, I could begin to focus on my next goal: Becoming debt-free in 12 months. Though I was eager to get the debt cleared, I found myself at a standstill. At-home training was approximately three weeks, and I was homeless by choice. I needed access to a house with a strong wifi signal. John Williams, who is also my unit shop supervisor, military mentor, and very close friend, opened his home up to me. John worked during the day, thus allowing me to have his home alone to train on this simulator without distractions. John extended his invitation to allow me to stay overnight when needed for early morning simulated flights.

It is every little boy's dream to fly drones. I had been fascinated by aircraft all my life, which is why I joined the Air Force. My Air Force experience and intelligence and the surveillance and reconnaissance experience I gained from my previous company made it relatively easy to transition over to the drone platform. The training for the flight crew was the most challenging experience of my life. Using a simulator, learning how to fly, taking daily quizzes and weekly tests without failure was a lot. I knew I would eventually pass and make it to flight line training, but that day seemed so far in the distance. July 26, 2019, I graduated as a certified Flight Crew Chief, Mission Coordinator, and Aircraft Operator for the Aerosonde MK 4.7 Unmanned Aircraft Vehicle (UAV).

Chapter Eleven

SNOWBALLING DEBT WITH SETBACKS

Shortly after graduating, I was sent back to Afghanistan. This time around, I was sent to the Dahlke, also known as Shank (Rocket City), the worst place in Afghanistan. The threat level in this area was extremely high. Each day, there was a minimum of five rockets shot at the base from the enemy. The alarm sounded, "INCOMING TAKE COVER NOW!" just a few hours after my arrival. I was scared, afraid, and uncertain if I really wanted to be there for that job anymore. Several vehicle-borne improvised explosive device (VBIED) attacks occurred at our entry gate to the base. These VBIED's were designed to be packed, placed, and detonated in a vehicle, injuring or killing anything in its vicinity. I remember feeling the shock wave of a VBIED attack that occurred while at work. The VBIED detonated on a military convoy just outside the base, killing many people. I prayed multiple times during the day, asking God for His protection over my life.

On July 10, 2019, prior to graduating UAV flight school, I was diagnosed with vertigo at St. Francis Medical Center-Emergency Department. Vertigo is the feeling of you moving when you're not, very similar to motion sickness. I had two insurance, employers insurance and Tri-care selective reserve insurance with the military. I was very confident between the two insurances my ER visit was covered, I would not occur any out of pocket expenses. Due to my condition, I was not able to operate any aircraft for the remainder of that week. August 18, 2019, to my surprise, I received a ER bill of over $2,200. This bill ruined my initial plans for snowballing my debt.

While deployed, the military covered my meals and lodging, and I didn't have to pay for utilities or anything like that. I contributed 30% of each paycheck to my company's savings plan, and the rest went towards my student loan debt. I took the $9k from my Bitcoin investment and started snowballing my debt. The debt snowballing method is a reduction strategy in which you make the minimum payments on all debt while aggressively attacking the smallest debt, thus paying it off first. I had three loans, and starting with the smallest loan, I began paying it down bi-weekly. I devoted most of my income to debt until I paid everything off.

My grandfather had been sick around this time, and he needed stents inserted into blocked arteries to keep them open. During the stenting procedure, he flatlined twice and had to be shocked three times to be brought back to life. He had over 95% blockage and almost needed open-heart surgery. I immediately took emergency leave and flew back across the world to check on him. While on leave, I had to stop making payments on my student loans because I was unsure how long I would be home. I refused to return to work until I knew his health had improved.

Fortunately, the company I worked for was understanding. My site lead instructed me to stay home and take as much time as I needed with my grandfather. Two weeks later, he was doing well and made a full recovery. I returned to work overseas to continue snowballing my debt.

After two months of sacrifice and dedication to my goal, my debt balance decreased, and I could see the light at the end of the tunnel. Also, when I returned, the season was shifting from fall to winter. Thankfully, our enemies fired fewer rockets when it was cold, as they don't prefer to be outside in the winter. The number of rockets per day decreased, and I started to feel at ease.

When I started making headway on my debt, another unfortunate, unexpected situation occurred: I was removed and barred from Afghanistan on Thanksgiving Day. During my time at Shank, I was allegedly disrespectful and hostile with the associated Operation Centers and other individuals culminating in refusal services, which had a severe and disruptive impact on combat operations. First, the allegations were simply untrue. I had always been polite, professional, and respectful in my interactions with the Operations Center personnel. Furthermore, at no time did I refuse services. During my conversations, I merely informed the individual of the weather conditions, forecast, and the probable impacts on the day's mission due to the Aerosonde Unmanned Aircraft's inability to fly in those conditions at the time, all in accordance with the company's contractual rights and obligations. Being permanently barred from the theater impacted my employment and my plans to become debt-free.

Once again, I had to stop payment on my student loans for an unforeseen amount of time. I held the money I had allocated for my student loan payments because things were uncertain. I was on edge and fell into a state of depression again. I felt like I was wrongly punished. My goals were clear, and I wouldn't do anything that crazy to jeopardize my plans. The allegations against me didn't even make sense.

There I was, without income and unable to fulfill my goal of becoming debt-free. My company requested that my installation bar be rescinded immediately, but the military denied the request. No one wins when it comes to the military. Two months later, I was reassigned to a different position in the Mediterranean Sea. My company flew me to our corporate headquarters office in Hunt Valley, MD. I met with the program manager, project manager, program plan and control analyst, and HR business unit. I toured the facilities and visited the lab where Aerosonde is tested. We revisited the unfortunate situation that took place in Afghanistan, and they thanked me for remaining professional throughout the process. On January 28, 2020, I arrived off the coast of the Mediterranean. I was excited to get back to work and get closer to becoming debt-free. I immediately continued with snowballing my debt. February came, and it was time to file yearly taxes with the IRS. When I received my tax refund check, it went directly towards attacking my debt. At this point, I was snowballing my debt with great intensity!

Chapter Twelve

TACKLING DEBT IN A PANDEMIC

March 2020 came and lasted for what felt like months. The Coronavirus (COVID-19) was spreading uncontrollably, sending us into a global pandemic. This global pandemic had everyone freaking out. Everything was uncertain, and all businesses were closed, with the exception of essential businesses like grocery stores and pharmacies. Yet again, I had to stop making payments on my student loans. I was not sure if Congress was going to forgive some or all of my student loan debt. Thankfully, my interest rates went to zero due to the pandemic.

As the pandemic worsened, our base went on lockdown, and we were only allowed to leave for groceries. Masking up and wearing gloves were the new norm. Hand sanitizer, bleach, Isopropyl Alcohol, hand soap, and other cleaning agents were in high demand. Somehow, toilet paper also became a high demand, leaving store shelves across the world empty. Food was scarce, and the price for food increased tremendously. At one point, grocery store shelves were almost empty. We were instructed to stock up on dry goods, and once our supplies were depleted, we would start eating MRE's (Meals Ready to Eat). MRE's are gross, and I would rather go without eating before opening MRE. Thank God the food never ran out. We were able to continue buying groceries at the grocery store and cooking our meals.

Many nonessential businesses were forced to close to minimize the spread of Covid-19. These businesses were closed for months, leaving some with no choice but to file for bankruptcy. Other companies relied on loans or government assistance. Airports and airlines were closing globally, restricting domestic and international travel to citizens and emergencies only. Stock market prices plummeted, and I knew I needed to take advantage of this opportunity.

By May 2020, I had maxed out my company's savings plan contribution for the year at $19,500 and had previously maxed out the contribution for 2019. Roth IRA and Rollover IRA were both maxed out, contributing $6k per account. All accounts were through Fidelity Investments. I used all $12k from both the Roth IRA and Rollover IRA to invest in the stock market, and I was on track to building a better portfolio. 40% of my paycheck biweekly was now going back to my net pay since I had maxed out the company's savings plan contributions. With this extra money, I could start back snowballing debt or buying more stocks. One stimulus check was direct deposited into my account, and that check went directly to my debt. I also received a 3% Merit Increase due to my work performance. This pay increase helped me get one step closer to reaching my goal.

Chapter Thirteen

THE ROAD LESS TRAVELED

On July 23, 2020, I made my final student loan payment to Great Lakes. I couldn't believe that I had paid off $88,167 of student loan debt in 12 months. Any minimum payments I made prior to July 26, 2019, only satisfied positive payment progression. Interests accrued daily, thus costing me more money over time. Therefore, my process of becoming debt-free really didn't start until after I graduated flight school. I always thought my proudest achievement would be the moment I made the final payment. When I finally made that last payment, I realized it was everything I'd done to get to that point that made me the proudest. I was proud of the choices and sacrifices I made to get to July 23, 2020.

After I became debt-free, I knew I had to create a new plan and goal. My friend, David, often told me to come up with a plan so that I would not be overseas forever. I had been using my income to knock out my debt, but with my debt paid off, I had to create a new plan for my money.

I listened to several audiobooks such as *Change Your Habits, Change Your Life: Strategies that Transformed 177 Average People into Self-Made Millionaires* by Tom Corley, *Unfu*k Yourself* by Gary John Bishop, *Everyday Millionaires* by Chris Hogan, *The 4-Hour Workweek: Escape 9-5, Live Anywhere, and Join The New Rich* by Timothy Ferriss, *Money Master the Game* by Tony Robbins, *Think and Grow Rich* by Napoleon Hill, *Million Dollar Habits* by Stellan Moreira, *The Book on Rental Property Investment* by Brandon Turner, and many more. These audiobooks all had an impact on my journey and gave me insight into what to do next. Having multiple streams of income and making money while I slept was ideal. I knew investing in rental properties would work well for me. David owns many rental properties and has done well for his business while working for his employer. He has been my mentor all this time, and I knew that if this were something I was willing to commit to, David would mentor me.

On September 11, 2020, I went to the U.S. Embassy in Beirut, Lebanon, to have an Alabama Durable Power of Attorney (POA) notarized. This POA would authorize David to make decisions concerning my properties. If David could not act for me, then his wife Sarah Rose Wallace would in his place. Later that afternoon, I completed my business plan, and the rental property business, HarrisCo Properties, LLC, was officially established.

Finding a real estate agent, property manager, mortgage professional, real estate attorney, insurance agent, home inspector, appraiser, accountant, maintenance contractor, and real estate mentor was easy. My experiences with buying and selling my home coupled with networking through David allowed me to build lasting relationships. Sarah Rose Wallace, now the owner of Wallace RPM, is my agent and property manager. On October 30, 2020, I closed on my first rental property in Montgomery, AL, and it was occupied when I purchased it. Later, on December 14, 2020, I purchased my second rental property that I would list as a short-term rental under AirBNB.

As I continued in my career, I planned to use my income to support my business, invest, tithe, and build wealth. The plan was to buy more properties, single-family homes, duplexes, and apartment complexes. Eventually, I wanted to invest in international properties.

As you can see, before I even considered investing or becoming debt-free, I had to change my mindset and the way I viewed money. Reading books on finances and listening to audiobooks and podcasts got me on the right path. My plan to become debt-free was a bit different from most. Since I was single with no children, selling everything and pursuing my contracting career overseas was easy. Staying healthy and physically fit helped me stay the course. I said this to say, what worked for me may not work for others. However, I wanted to share my story to let you know that becoming debt-free is possible.

No matter what your goal is, it will require you to make sacrifices. Along my journey to becoming debt-free, I had to sacrifice starting my own family, daily putting my life in danger, missing family reunions, births, birthdays, weddings, and holidays. Breaking the generational curse and becoming debt-free was once a dream, but my decisions and sacrifices made it my reality.

I had many setbacks, but my comeback was much stronger. Budgeting my income every month and giving every dollar a mission required a lot of focus and intentionality, but it was worth it. I am currently 31 and debt-free, working every day to become a millionaire. I am not a product of my circumstances; I am a product of my choices. I chose to be a better me for my future, and I'm glad I did.

As you pursue your journey to becoming debt-free, or whatever is in your heart to do, be careful not to underestimate the power of consistency, determination, and wise choices. You have what it takes to make the choices to become the best version of yourself. Strength does not come from what you can do; it comes from overcoming the things you once thought you could not! God surely has guided my path every step of the way, and I truly thank Him for my life, the plan He has for me, and for every person He placed on my path to aid me on my journey. God is my provider, and I genuinely believe that because He could trust me to manage a little well, He has blessed me with more than I have room to receive!

If you live like no one else, later you can live like no one else.

-Dave Ramsey

MEET THE AUTHOR

Hailing from the rural community of Highland Home, AL, Corey Harris is an accomplished and disciplined man on a mission to help others experience financial freedom. In 2008, Corey graduated from Highland Home High School and set out for Alabama Agricultural and Mechanical University. As a first-generation college student with very few scholarships to support his undergraduate and graduate tuition, Corey persevered and obtained both a Bachelor of Science and Master of Science from his beloved AAMU. Later, Corey earned his teacher's certification from Athens State University and taught Agriculture Science within Montgomery Public Schools District. Even with two degrees and a certification under his belt, Corey struggled financially until he decided to make some major decisions, including selling the major assets he had purchased as an adult, to tackle the debt he had accrued over the years.

Corey currently serves as an aircraft operator, flying unmanned aircraft systems in restricted international airspace for Textron Systems. Though it is a demanding career, his duty does not keep him from pursuing his purpose and passions. Since reclaiming his financial freedom, he has been on a mission to encourage and inspire others to do the same. It is Corey's hope that his first book, Breaking the Generational Curse: My Journey to Becoming Debt Free, ignites readers to develop the resilience to commit to debt repayment strategies and create a suitable plan for life after debt.

When he's not considering his next wealth investment, Corey enjoys traveling, working out, and encouraging others to create the life they desire. He also finds pleasure in sowing into the community, and as a proud member of Alpha Phi Alpha Fraternity, Inc., he is never void of an opportunity to give back. In the near future, Corey plans to develop more opportunities to connect with others through encouraging financial freedom as well as other budding business endeavors.

STAY CONNECTED

Thank you for reading, *Breaking the Generational Curse: My Journey to Becoming Debt Free*. Corey looks forward to connecting with you. Here are a few ways you can connect with the author and stay updated on new releases, speaking engagements, products, and more.

FACEBOOK   COREY A. HARRIS
INSTAGRAM   @coreyaharris
WEBSITE   www.coreyaharris.net
TWITTER   @coreyaharris

www.ingramcontent.com/pod-product-compliance
Lightning Source LLC
Chambersburg PA
CBHW030201100526
44592CB00009B/387